anythink

SPORTS FOR SPROUTS

CHEERLEADING

Holly Karapetkova

ROURKE PUBLISHING

Vero Beach, Florida 32964

www.rourkepublishing.com

Photo credits: All photography by Renee Brady for Blue Door Publishing, except Cover © Wendy Nero; Title Page © Wendy Nero, Crystal Kirk, Leah-Anne Thompson, vnosokin, Gerville Hall, Rob Marmion; Page 12 © Robert J. Daveant; Page 14 © Tony Wear; Sidebar Silhouettes © Sarah Nicholl

Editor: Meg Greve

Cover and page design by Nicola Stratford, Blue Door Publishing

Acknowledgements: Thank you to *Funtastic Cheerleading* and the Gemini Cheerleaders for their assistance on this project

Library of Congress Cataloging-in-Publication Data

Karapetkova, Holly.
  Cheerleading / Holly Karapetkova.
     p. cm. -- (Sports for sprouts)
  ISBN 978-1-60694-322-9 (hard cover)
  ISBN 978-1-60694-822-4 (soft cover)
  ISBN 978-1-60694-563-6 (bilingual)
  1. Cheerleading--Juvenile literature. I. Title.
  LB3635.K37 2009
  791.6'4--dc22
                                                                    2009002254

Rourke Publishing
Printed in the United States of America, North Mankato, Minnesota
072710
072610LP-B

ROURKE PUBLISHING

www.rourkepublishing.com - rourke@rourkepublishing.com
Post Office Box 643328 Vero Beach, Florida 32964

I am a cheerleader.

3

4

I cheer for a football team. I am on a **squad**.

We wear uniforms with
our team's name
and colors.

We do **cheers**.

We clap our hands.

We can do **buckets** and **candlesticks**.

We can do **cartwheels** and jumps.

We learn **routines**. We move together and stay in line.

Sometimes we use pom-poms.

We always smile, even when we make mistakes.

Glossary

buckets (BUH-kits): Sometimes cheerleaders hold their arms in buckets. They put their arms straight in front or to the sides and turn their fists down like they are holding buckets.

candlesticks (KAN-duhl-stiks): Cheerleaders hold their arms in candlesticks. They put their arms out straight in front with their fists turned sideways, like they are holding candlesticks.

cartwheels (KART-weels): Cartwheels are tumbling moves cheerleaders do to excite the crowd. It is done by raising your arms straight over your head and then putting your hands on the ground. At the same time, swing both legs over one after the other.

cheers (CHIHRZ): Cheers are longer than chants and have movements, words, tumbles, and stunts.

routines (roo-TEENZ): Routines are long series of cheers, movements, dances, tumbles, and stunts. Sometimes cheerleaders perform routines to music.

squad (SKWAHD): A squad is a group of cheerleaders. A squad works together to cheer for a sports team.

23

Index

Websites

www.unitedcheer.com

uca.varsity.com

www.cheerwiz.com

About The Author

Holly Karapetkova, Ph.D., loves writing books and poems for kids and adults. She teaches at Marymount University and lives in the Washington, D.C., area with her husband, her son K.J., and her two dogs, Muffy and Attila.